The Black Woman's Guide to Advancing in Academia

DR. JENNIFER J. EDWARDS
DR. NDIDI AMUTAH-ONUKAGHA

The Black Woman's Guide to Advancing in Academia

© 2019 Upstream LLC

ISBN: 978-1-970079-47-0

Publisher: Upstream LLC
Formatting and editing: Opportune Independent Publishing Company

Welcome!

Navigating academia as a professor offers an opportunity to build a prestigious career and transform the knowledge and attitudes of today's students. This book equips Black women and those interested in teaching at a college or university with the tools to consider the best academic setting, define effective topics for teaching, consider and understand the realities of academia, and make your next move. You can turn the tide on your career in academia, whether you are submitting a competitive job application or strategically deciding the next steps in your tenure pursuit.

Twelve notable Black women professors will share their stories, successes and hurdles regarding advancing in academia. We share this collection of stories to spark inspiration and remind you that the path of success within the academy is certainly attainable for you. No two stories or lives are the same. Each path to enter and succeed in academia is different. This *Black Woman's Guide* offers keen and timely wisdom about advancing in academia. By reading this guide you will gain critical insights on becoming a competitive faculty member, promotion, work-life integration, as well as race, gender, and intersectionality and their influence on the Black woman's faculty experience.

The two editors met over ten years ago at a training at the Brookings Institution in Washington, DC. We are national Pan-Hellenic greek sisters, who pursued parallel careers in public health and have had the pleasure of staying in touch over time. When you meet someone with similar and drive and goals, you stay connected. We want to share our energy and further empower ladies who are proficient in this field. This guide is intended to help you learn effective strategies to give you the inside track to landing an interview and advancing successfully in your career. Get ready for a straightforward, actionable, transparent conversation about advancing in academia. We're here to equip you to teach, earn, and advance in academia. Enjoy!

Together in the journey,

Dr. Jennifer J. Edwards
Dr. Ndidiamaka N. Amutah-Onukagha
Co-Editors, *The Black Woman's Guide to Advancing in Academia*

Table of Contents

Where To Start

Guest lecturing is a great way to jumpstart your career in academia. Guest lecturing means you get to take over a professor's class and teach their students. The benefits of guest lecturing are that you can focus on a topic that is of special importance to you and speak passionately about it to an audience of students who are engaged. It's important to reflect on your interests—choose courses that are of interest to you and that relate to your professional experiences. With guest lectures, you gain teaching experience, practice in managing a classroom and facilitating dialogue, and the classes can be added to your resume to demonstrate your capability for future faculty applications.

Guest lectures are also a great way to build relationships with departments that may be hiring in the future. They will know who you are and may share information and invitations for future faculty hiring opportunities.

When entering the classroom, keep in mind that the students have never seen you before and you are offering them new information. You have never given them an exam or graded their homework. They are simply a captive audience that you get to expand your teaching skills with. Guest lectures are often guided with powerpoint slides that include videos as well as interactive discussion, with plenty of time for questions. You are likely representing the perspective of a professional from the field in which they would like to work in one day. You have the chance to share your heart and expertise as an example for those entering your particular field in the future.

Guest lecturing is also a helpful way to determine the school profile – faculty and student characteristics, mission alignment, and other school features – that works best for your own preferences. When applying for faculty positions it is important to consider that each institution has its own personality. You want to enter into a journey that aligns with your beliefs, instructional skills, and goals. Consider whether a state or a private institution fits your needs best. Would you want to serve at a historically black college or university (HBCU), religious institution, or university focusing specifically on certain student needs like the deaf community? Would you thrive better at a community college or a four-year commuter school? How large of a university and what size classroom would you be most successful in? Gain clarity on the institutional profile that works best for you. There is no room for compromise in this area, as it can often affect how you interact with students, acceptable conversations in the classroom, as well as your own professional and personal schedule.

What is the best way to get started with guest lecturing? Start with your professional relationships. Do you know someone on faculty already at the local community college, college, or university? If so, ask them if you can join them in their classroom one day. If not, reach out to the local institutions to see if their relevant departments have an interest in guest lectures. Put together a solid CV, research philosophy, and teaching statement to reach out directly to department chairs. If faculty member names and their courses (or at least research areas) are listed, e-mail faculty members who mirror your interests directly, as they will likely be teaching a course that could benefit from your guest lecture. E-mail addresses are often publicly listed on the departmental webpages. It's as simple as that. Just ask.

Creating Competitive Application Materials

What atmosphere and experience will you create for your students? Your teaching philosophy is a vital guide that illustrates your classroom operations, standards, and energy. It reflects your values, personality, brand, and priorities. The teaching philosophy illustrates what you find to be most important in the classroom and how you will execute and maintain appropriate strategies to ensure you practice what is enclosed in the statement. The philosophy defines expectations for how you will engage with your students and how you will manage your classroom.

The teaching philosophy is a core document to develop for your competitive faculty application. Some applicants are unaware of the importance of this collateral, but now you know that it is truly a feature of a standout submission. Your philosophy must convey three to four, definitely no more than five, key areas of focus. It should have a strong opener that connects to the mission of the university to which you are applying. The philosophy is written in first person and includes the general topic area as a header, then may reference the opportunities or challenges for context, followed by your proposed solutions and strategies. The teaching philosophy should not exceed one typewritten page.

Though not always required during the application process, teaching philosophies increase your competitiveness as an applicant to any category of a faculty position, whether full-time, part-time, or online. Submit yours as an additional attachment even if it is not requested. Reason being, it conveys core attributes of your values and they are actually not as likely to change much over time—

though always allow yourself the flexibility to update it as you desire.

Some additional considerations regarding the classroom include understanding your teaching load and schedule. How many courses will you teach per term? Meaning, you may have one course for which you teach two or three sections. Or, you may have three courses for which you teach one section. Each unique course requires course preparation, exam preparation, lecture preparation, and of course, student engagement. The time invested directly relates to the number of courses you will have, as well as your ability to navigate between distinct subject matter covered in each course. Also, consider how many classes you will teach per day? Many professors find that they hit a wall if three classes are taught within the same day, no matter if it is the same course or not. What are your own limitations, strengths, and preferences?

Your Teaching Philosophy

Several extracted values from a real teaching philosophy are as follows: Use this as a guide to think about what is most important to you as a professor. But remember, you must be you and develop your own teaching statement. Your interview panel will see right through you if you have submitted anything unauthentic. Think about the values and strategies where you are strongest and discuss what you most believe in. Here are sample values from a teaching philosophy. Note that it is worded to reflect your personal views and utilizing first person is common. The teaching philosophy is a personal statement of your approach to leading in the classroom.

Engagement

To engage students in the classroom, I encourage a variety of projects, critiques and reviews, presentations, reading, writing, and other activities to address the various learning needs of the class.

These projects and activities can often be tailored to the issues of interest to the student, while still meeting departmental and university requirements.

Accountability

A strong work ethic characterizes the leadership development of students, which begins in the classroom. I value accountability in the classroom and do not support excuses; however, be mindful that the circumstances of students can emerge that may legitimately preclude a student from full participation. I am an ongoing advocate for students and works with them during times of extenuating circumstances where the student has otherwise demonstrated accountability and a sound work ethic.

Interaction

I believe in being accessible to students that need assistance outside of the class time, including one-on-one online (or in-person) sessions during office hours, and the use of new technology to communicate with classes or students as needed. Interaction is closely linked to engagement in the classroom and extends beyond the classroom to include faculty accessibility and student support. Furthermore, I believe in the respectful engagement of students with each other and with me to foster interest and excitement. *end of statement*

To increase your competitiveness, your philosophy should specifically speak to how you will leverage your faculty role as full-time, part-time, or online to be an asset to your students. You must identify the challenges and opportunities within your specified capacity and define values that will allow you to best serve as a faculty member. For example, adjunct or part-time faculty members should address their accessibility in their philosophy since you are not present on campus all of the time. Full-time faculty members can address how they may integrate their lessons from research into the classroom and grow students to become interested in further study. You must develop your own philosophy to illustrate your tailored approach to serving on faculty. Your sincerity in your philosophy will be apparent in interviews and it must reflect your own individual strengths as a resource for students in the in-person or online classroom.

Pursuing Research and the Research Statement

Consider how your research fits in with the overall and departmental faculty profile. How does your research align with and complement the goals of the department to which you are applying? Are there other faculty members within and across the department(s) that could become future co-investigators? Or, will there be a challenging element of competition in a case where your research overlaps too closely with someone already on faculty?

Also, consider whether or not you will have what you need to be successful in pursuing further research. Is the department allocating and paying you for research or is it considered above and beyond teaching responsibilities? Is there a graduate degree program within the department that have graduate students that can offer research assistance for you? If you feel this all aligns with your research goals, proceed with completing your application and research statement.

Developing a solid research statement sets applicants apart from the rest. Research statements are a vital component of full-time and tenure track faculty positions. It is also helpful content to supplement applications for faculty positions that may involve optional research responsibilities. The research statement is your platform to convey how your knowledge and expertise will revolutionize the industry that you are in.

Research for the sake of research is passé and not impactful. Research statements must illustrate how your unique approach to solving problems as well as your innovative solutions set you apart from other applicants. Your approach to solving problems demonstrates your creativity in the design of efficient and effective methods. Your innovative solutions represent the funding potential your research has. You must demonstrate that you can bring additional funds into the institution where you are applying.

While you are writing the research statement from the perspective of how your work makes a difference in your industry and society, the hiring committee is reviewing it for competitiveness in landing sustainable grant funds for their department first and foremost. Department and college leadership must consider the business and financial implications of faculty decisions, and it's the future faculty member's ethical responsibility to assure that their own research profile is benevolent. Of course, it remains everyone's responsibility to assure the responsible conduct of research and your research statement should illustrate clear understanding of these core human subjects and ethical principles.

Tactically speaking, depending on the institution, your research statement may be a separate file or it may have to be content that is incorporated into your cover letter. If it is part of a cover letter, the research statement should be integrated into a letter that does not exceed two pages. The cover letter should start with standard cover letter language thanking the selection committee for reviewing your application, and then transition into an empowered discussion of your research. Your research should be presented as an added value to the institution, college, and departmental research profile. Whether as part of a cover letter or a standalone statement, your introduction should convey knowledge of their current work and illustrate how your research fits into their research landscape.

The research statement then addresses the three premier research areas where you can best contribute to growing the department to which you are applying. These three research areas may represent overlapping concepts within your overall research, or they may reflect three separate research areas where you have proven results by way of papers and presentations.

The three areas should not be totally disparate and should complement each other or build upon each other. For example, research on breast cancer screening among women in rural areas may be broken down into discussion in your research statement pertaining to breast cancer, screening, and rural areas if you are choosing complementary topics within one focused research theme you have had throughout your career.

On the other hand, if this is one of the diverse studies you have had on similar topics, you may craft your research statements around the three core areas of women's health, chronic disease, and rural health. This gives you latitude to contribute to a range of research while demonstrating that you still have some focus. If you are in fields such as sciences or engineering, your research statement will likely be the former. If you are in fields such as sociology or public health, your research statement would likely align with the latter.

Discuss your successes in each of the three areas, illustrate why the topic areas are vital to the field, and inject your personal values where appropriate to convey your passion for the research. Highlight the three subject areas with subheadings that are italicized or underlined to support a focused approach to covering the content.

In general, research statements can effectively be conveyed in a few pages. Now, you will have your cover letter that may be one page, plus your teaching philosophy that should be up to one page, then your research statement of 2-3 pages, and of course your CV. Visit our website for a sample faculty application for inspiration that rose to the top of 100 applicants and received a job offer.

Close out your research statement with the final appeal for why you are a competitive applicant for the position. Research statements are critical to demonstrate why you are the missing puzzle piece to the faculty to which you are applying. No two research statements are the same, and it is your opportunity to shine.

Your Curriculum Vitae

The curriculum vitae (CV) represents the roster of your career success. It differs from a resume in that it offers more details on your professional experiences, and has dedicated sections to discuss research, presentation, and funding—aspects of academia that are vital for the faculty selection committee to consider. A strong vitae's longest section is typically publications, followed by presentations. Also, the more funds that you have brought in, the better. If you are applying for adjunct positions, a strong resume illustrating vital professional experience will likely suffice.

Your CV should naturally demonstrate alignment with your research statement, and it should certainly reflect any past experience in academia or education that you have had. There are various ways to organize a CV, and oftentimes upon hire, there are specific formats that may be unique to your university that they will expect you to report in for promotion and tenure consideration. For the sake of your application, your CV should include the following components: chronology of education, certifications, research interests list, qualifications summary statement, chronology of employment, honors and awards, service to the field (volunteering, reviewer roles, etc.), service to the university (committees, program etc.), publications, presentations, and memberships. Every section is not mandatory, but sections should reflect your past experiences and success. Stylistically, use action statements and words, quantify your wins, and use classic and clean fonts that are appropriate for academia.

The Classroom Climate

Let's talk about grit. Grit is an inherent characteristic that is needed to enter and advance in academia. Grit is needed to withstand the competitive application process and withstand the classroom environment. It is also needed to endure the challenges that occur among faculty. Every black woman in academia must have this vital quality. Grit represents the balance of being classy yet tough and gracious yet firm.

First, let's talk about the armor we need to wear when we are applying to full-time, part-time, and online positions in academia. We can then address the challenges and opportunities to navigate classroom struggles and challenges with fellow faculty. Gracious grit is needed all along the way.

The applicant pool for positions in academia is always vast.. Depending on the level of competitiveness of the brick-and-mortar university you are seeking out, the applicant pool could also be worldwide or at least nationwide and particularly in the case of Ivy League institutions and large state universities. This means we must put our best foot forward during the application process and our guide will offer significant resources to help you do that. Applicant pools for the adjunct and part-time positions are also competitive in that they contain applicants that do and do not have a terminal degree, and spend their time in the field as professionals who also want to teach. There is a different level of competitiveness to enter academia through this path.

Once you enter into academia there is a level of toughness that is required in order for you to sustain in the classroom setting. Students are incredible at insulting their professor when they can and cannot take advantage of a situation. Therefore we have to balance the grace that we offer our students, including those that have sensitivities, with the firmness that is required to engage in effective classroom management. Also, ensure that the department in which you seek to teach educates students that have career aspirations relating to your interest area.

Professors are gifted at reading the room. On the first day, we can often discern those students who will be most and least engaged. Students are also conducting their own assessment of their professors. It is safe to say that we all have implicit biases of some kind. We, professors and future professors, exercise the professionalism to bracket any potential bias, but students are not required to exercise this level of critical thinking when it comes to interpersonal interactions. As a result, students often treat us based on how they have judged us with the limited information they have about our character, passion, and educational capabilities. Also as women, sometimes we face the negative attitudes of those who think women are inferior.

As Black women, we can face the challenges of those who believe we are inferior due to our race. There are also implicit biases where professors of older age may receive more respect than younger professors; however, it can be difficult to discern which bias is at play given the intersectionality of these three identities: race, gender, and age. Therefore, keep the grit and stay true to your passion to be in the classroom regardless of the attitudes, challenges, or sometimes outright racially motivated poor behavior that you may be on the receiving end of. It is definitely the exception, not the rule, but it is a consistent reality. Let's connect with some real-life stories and reflections of Black women in academia.

Advancing in Academia:
12 Inspirational Stories from the Field

Twelve notable Black women professors share their stories, successes, hurdles regarding advancing in academia. No two stories are the same. Each path to enter and succeed in academia is different. This *Black Woman's Guide* offers wisdom about advancing in the equally competitive, yet rewarding, environment that is academia. By reading this book you will gain critical insights concerning becoming a competitive faulty applicant, promotion, work-life integration, as well as race, gender, and intersectionality and their influence on the Black woman's faculty experience. Here are their unique journeys, personal perceptions, and first-hand accounts of their careers in academia. These ladies are leading by example.

A Master's Degree Path

Halima E. Curry, MPH, MPT, has over 15 years of experience as a physical therapist and almost 3 years of experience as an adjunct instructor at Baker College-Allen Park (Allen Park, MI) as a part of the Physical Therapist Assistant Program. Clinical and academic education has been her focus and will continue to be as she is a recent graduate of the MPH program at the University of Michigan-Flint. Although her career trajectory has not been conventional or seamless, it has been beneficial to the teachings of the clinicians and students that she has taught.

Thoughts on advancing in academia from Halima: I was an adjunct instructor at Baker College of Allen Park for two and a half years in the health sciences department. I enjoyed teaching my patients regarding their health conditions and treatment regimen, as well as student physical therapists in their professional growth. I was able to establish professional rapport with the program director at Baker College who was in need of an adjunct instructor for their Introduction to PT course and continued from there with minimal experience. I currently work in a clinical/hospital setting and are able to take students in that setting to apply their academic knowledge to clinical and real-life experiences. I have also recently completed my MPH in health education which places a new realm of knowledge to my current PT position to be able to apply it to the public health profession.

What is truly inspiring is when a student is able to take the knowledge they have learned and gain success, whether it is on an exam or just the smile on their faces when they learn something new or are inspired by a concept they've learned. What energizes me is being able to research or investigate a new technique to assist a class, or an individual student, in learning a technique or concept. I would define success as a state of personal and professional growth and balance. Also, success is being able to be in a profession or having a sense of accomplishment that gives a person complete peace knowing that they are in the chosen field with or without any financial or professional gain attached. My path entering academia was purely by happenstance and seizing opportunities based on my skills and talents. Although, there may have been some hereditary influence, as my mother is a retired educator.

The school in which I taught was a small, public, commuter, community college. The positives for that was that most students were motivated by working, families, etc. which made them want to learn the information so that they could provide for themselves and their families in a relatively short period of time. I found this beneficial in teaching because many were motivated beyond just obtaining their degree. Additionally, many of the students were non-traditional in age because they had to work or had families at a young age which hindered them from coming to college right out of high school. This was a good choice for me because my career trajectory was not necessarily seamless. I think schools that have some non-traditional categories of student population suits me well.

My advice to entering into the academy is to be direct, professionally transparent, and meet students as well as faculty peers where they are. This will help garner respect and trust.

The only hurdle that I can recall from performance evaluations is that there is always one student who does not take your teaching methods favorably. It can be discouraging, however, I take note of it and try not to repeat the situation—(provided it is constructive in nature).

Thankfully, there have not been any hindrances as a woman faculty member. However, I have encountered some apprehension by being an African American faculty member and instructor. I believe because of the area that the school was located and the racial makeup of the community caused some difficulties at times in the faculty and teaching process.

As an adjunct instructor, I was able to work full time which was a challenge at times. The time needed for preparation and grading in addition to working and personal commitments were difficult at times to balance. Time management was key and utilizing the time that I was at school wisely was paramount because the school was located at least 40 minutes away from my home.

I believe that with each year and each class that I taught, I learned something new about myself, my teaching abilities, and new approaches to teaching different students and audiences. My advice for a new female faculty member is to stay true to yourself, remain fair in the intent and grading, and do not be afraid to take a risk in a teaching activity or project. Seeing students after going through my class that have found jobs and advanced professionally as a result of the teachings in my class has been a great success. Even though it was a foundational course, it still makes me proud to have a part in their success.

My career trajectory has not been conventional or seamless, however, I have been able to utilize my skills and talents in the academic realm and to teach students effectively. My main advice is to stay true to who you are at the core and that will come through your teaching. Black and brown women are moving forward and upward in all types of careers and I hope this book helps to inspire those looking to move into academia and all careers that serve people.

Technologist in Academia

Dr. Henrietta Okoro is an associate professor and lead software test engineer. She has spent nine years in academia and 25 years in information technology (IT). She serves as a university associate professor, and commissioner on the Governor's Commission on African Affairs (GCOAA), Maryland, USA. She is also founder and president of the World Association for Academic Doctors (WAAD), Inc. and founder and CEO of the Association of Nigerian Women Academic Doctors (ANWAD), Inc.. She entered academia with the main goal to share knowledge and continue to widen knowledge in academics and technology.

Seeing her students attain their highest potential gives her energy. She enjoys helping students to develop and enhance their skills and career path. According to Dr. Okoro, success is when an action produces a positive result. For example, inspiring someone to move to the next level from where he or she is. Also, to develop their untapped skills and attain the highest level. She collaborates and uses best practices to excel, empowers the underprivileged in the local and global community, and empowers women and girls' education in developing countries.

Thoughts on advancing in academia from Henrietta: I have both public and private school teaching experience. Both environments foster a commitment to a strong academic program and preparing students for ethical decision-making, integrating policy and research, to become moral leaders, and practice in the technologically advanced world. My job is to reassure students that a successful career requires dedication, hard work, and sacrifice.

Diversity and inclusion contribute to the issues of performance evaluation and promotion consideration in some organizations. Leadership and management skills are vital for organizations and thus should be considered as a prerequisite for the employee during performance evaluations rather than cultural differences. Maintaining excellence in performance is the key to success and exhibiting proven positive results to gain a competitive advantage among peers helps to overcome the hurdles of promotion.

Actually, neither gender nor race have had an impact as far as I am concerned. My faculty experience has worked well with all genders. My biggest challenge has been to finance and embark on my education and charity projects. My greatest successes are inspiring students to attain their career pursuit, mentoring my colleagues on securing employment, enhancing research skills, networking, and strong academic growth.

Time management and prioritization are the keys to managing challenges to maintain success. Entering into advance careers exposes one to several challenges. With new demands and expectations, one can be distracted. Applying effective time management and setting priority helps to overcome these challenges.

Effective communication, productivity, and managing boundaries are the key to success in life. Great leaders strive to send their message across. Keeping quiet will bury your ideas. Being productive shows results and keeps the business going. Managing boundaries helps to manage diversity inclusion. Successful leaders carry everyone along while maintaining commitments and setting goals.

Liberating Women in Academia

Jameta Nicole Barlow, Ph.D., MPH, a Charlottesville, Virginia native, is a community health psychologist and an assistant professor of writing at The George Washington University in Washington, DC. Dr. Barlow utilizes decolonizing methodologies to disrupt intergenerational trauma, chronic health diseases and structural policies adversely affecting Black girls' and women's health. She has spent nearly 20 years in transdisciplinary collaborations with physicians, public health practitioners, researchers, policy administrators, activists, political appointees, and community members in diverse settings.

She serves as the assistant professor of writing of the University Writing Program at The George Washington University. She has been in academia since 2010, including positions as assistant professor of writing, University Writing Program, Columbian College of Arts and Sciences, The George Washington University; assistant professor in Women and Health, Department of Women's and Gender Studies, Towson University; and others.

Thoughts on advancing in academia from Dr. Barlow: I come from a family of teachers and school administrators, but knew that teaching at the K-12 level was not for me. I remember working in the federal government and experiencing frustration at the discourse around the table. This table was filled with MDs and PhDs, but very few, if any, looked like me, a Southern Black woman, yet they were making decisions about health disparities in Black communities and other communities of color. Because at the time I only had an MPH, I knew that in order to contribute to the discourse I had to get a Ph.D. Over time, I fell in love with teaching and discovered how I could also contribute to transforming the landscape of health by teaching and mentoring future colleagues—how I choose to view my students.

I've recently returned to the nation's capital for a new professional position. In the past, I was typically involved with at least one local organization committed to social justice in areas such as food equity or women's health. However, most of my current efforts are in providing spaces for healing for community members, as a certified Emotional Emancipation Circle Facilitator. And, working in leadership positions within professional organizations such as the Council on Black Health.

Knowing that I'm contributing to the future liberation of women, health and social justice warriors committed to equity and the elimination of injustices inspires me. I love that moment…in the classroom, when you see the light bulb click for students. That feeling is addictive and motivation for me to continue to do this incredibly rewarding work.

Success is achieving your goals, regardless of what society, your family, and friends define as success. It is internal, relative and dependent upon that which brings an individual joy. Success requires self-awareness, which requires time spent with oneself. Only then can you self-define success. Being able to articulate your life's passion and purpose and achieving that passion and purpose is, in fact, success.

I fell into academia as I saw it as a way to use my standpoint to create better research, become an effective advocate and to nurture the next generation of scholar-activists-practitioners. I've taught at public, private and regional teaching universities. It is important to find a good fit for you, your personality and lifestyle. As a younger

Black woman, I often have students from other colleges seeking mentorship and a listening ear because there are so few faculty members of color. There are pros and cons to all types of schools. For me, because I was often the only Black person in the classroom, being integrated in my neighborhood and experiencing blatant and subtle acts of gendered racism, I'm deeply committed to being a resource to students in spaces such as these.

Students tend to appreciate my openness and honesty. My biggest piece of advice for them to understand is that they can create the life they want, despite the barriers. I encourage them to keep trying, despite the obstacles. And, to bring another person along as they continue to achieve. Create a community while creating your life.

I've been accused of inflating my grades when my students are genuinely and collectively improving, based on my Black feminist pedagogy and womanist praxis. I've also encountered colleagues within my department who were jealous of my "popularity" and sought to undermine it by speaking negatively about me to my students. Though I never sought promotion, I think it did have an impact on my routine performance evaluation. Still, I persisted. And it did not negatively impact my evaluation. These hurdles have reminded me of the precarious nature of Black women in the academy. Not only is it exhausting due to challenges by colleagues from privileged groups, but your allies can also often inflict similar acts of exhaustion, simply by minimizing your contribution to the department, college, and university.

You can overcome the hurdles as you pursue promotion by creating your community, making friends with staff and administrators, as well as other faculty. I learned how to overcome hurdles by doing such. Further, it prompted me to expand my networks. While I never went up for promotion and tenure, I was well placed to achieve it. Be sure to ask your future employer how they are actively addressing antiracist, antisexist and related behaviors in your classroom department, division, college, and university. It's important to understand how underrepresented faculty are protected from excessive service activities.

Intersectionality means that my social experiences are influenced by how society views and treats me based on my marginalized identities. It is a challenge to assign this solely to my gender, race, age, or any other identities. However, I do know that I've experienced ageism while working in high-level positions in the federal government and in having to manage staff twice my age. I also know that gendered racism contributed to my negative experience during my first doctoral program. I know now that not every institution appreciates and accepts my culture's cultivation of strong, confident, Southern Black women. I do believe this, in combination with my professional experience at the age of 25, was a challenge to my faculty in that institution. Gendered racism is problematic and dangerous because it minimizes the potential of women of color. As a result, the institution does not benefit from diverse perspectives and women of color, or Black women, such as myself, are socially exposed to micro and macro aggressions, further complicating the stressors we now know that contribute to cortisol levels. Thus, gendered racism is a structural determinant of health for Black women.

I have a strong commitment to myself and my family. Thus, we are prioritized above all else. By creating this boundary, I'm better able to navigate academia. For example, I devote certain days to writing and others to teaching. I'm committed to certain days for the physical activities I enjoy, such as dancing and yoga. Also, I have no problem saying to colleagues that I'm unavailable for events that conflict with family time.

My biggest challenge has been being okay with not listening or following the advice of mentors or colleagues who may have a vision for my career that is not consistent with the vision I have for my academic career. Ironically, my biggest success has been getting kicked out of my first Ph.D. program. It taught me perseverance, as well as serving as an instruction guide for how NOT to treat my students. I share my experience with students to motivate them— just because I was kicked out of a doctoral program, it doesn't mean I was stymied from completing a Ph.D. My first program was not a good fit and was a horrible experience. But I learned some amazing lessons and met equally amazing people. My second program was the perfect experience for me. There, I found my authentic voice as an academic, and my unique perspective to this work was celebrated. I also had an advisor/mentor who modeled what mentoring is supposed to look like and is a major reason why I'm still in academia.

My advice to Black women reading this book is to fly as high as you want. There are many people who may not support you but nourish your spirit and prepare yourself for the ride. It's beautiful and we need your unique perspective to radically change the face, heart, and spirit of academia. Remember that your mediocre is still most likely superior to others…because to get where you are today, in this society as a Black/Brown woman, you had to be the best. Keep shining and remember to bring someone along as you fly higher. Be your authentic self. That in itself is unique and will make your work stand out.

Success is a Feeling

Jennifer Edwards, Ph.D. leads a well company, serves as online adjunct healthcare administration graduate faculty, and is a principal research scientist at a national health nonprofit. She is a lifetime health advocate who is passionate about health equity and social action.

Thoughts on advancing in academia from Dr. Edwards: It's

wonderful working with non-traditional students who are returning to school to advance their careers. It presents its challenges as a younger Ph.D. mentoring people who are my parent's age, or successful leaders in their own right who are sometimes less coachable for that reason. In the end, they develop strong research, make a difference, and we get through the process together. My ten-year career in academia started as an instructor of record, graduate teaching assistant, at Howard University. They paid for my tuition and I gained valuable experience.

I then served first as a guest lecturer at a local state university, as well as an adjunct professor as I continued to build my career in public health. Then, I transitioned to a full-time lecturer position for about three years. Due to some barriers within the department, transitioning to tenure track was not a smart move on my part. There were no tenured professors in public health, and I'd be evaluated by professors outside of my discipline which was not ideal, preferred, or even standard. The pay was also poor, and they truly hired me at a lower level than I should have been, and I was too new to academia to know what the promotion progression was to make a smarter decision.

During this time, I began serving as a contributing graduate faculty for an online institution, which was a part-time commitment. I still maintain that commitment to date and have returned to working in the field as a researcher and coordinating an annual women's wellness event as my other sources of income. It's super important to maintain a diverse portfolio. Earning a doctoral degree allows that flexibility to take on multiple projects and truly leverage your expertise as a platform for fun and interesting paid projects.

I started as a graduate teaching assistant when I was working on my doctoral degree. Our department would pay our entire tuition if we taught one or two of the undergraduate classes. That was an offer that was tough to refuse, especially given how expensive student loans are to pay back for years to come. I actually resisted choosing academia beyond graduate school but found that I kept getting invited to speak for different audiences and that leaders in the community valued my opinion and began inviting me to guest lecture. From there I accepted that I may have some talent to educate and began the journey into academia. I believe adjunct instruction—online or in-person—will always be part of my life. I love inspiring and helping people achieve their dreams.

I also serve others through my work on nonprofit boards and give back to the field by reviewing for academic journals including U.S. Office of the Surgeon General's *Public Health Reports*. I have a natural inclination and passion for empowering women and girls, so much of my recreational time is spent on related efforts. I get to help ladies focus on self-care and truly recharge so we can continue serving those around us. We can't pour from an empty cup.

I really devote my time to health and education. Anything that falls outside of those two realms does not often get my attention. Different times of year are more intense for certain activities, and I devote specific days of the week to each effort, which has been my core to balancing it all. There is no such thing as multitasking. I'm all-in on whatever I'm doing at the time. My time and energy are limited and I like to focus on areas where I can best serve others.

I'm so inspired and I love it when a student gets it. Some students just want to get by. Other students just want an "A", but from time to time there is that student who truly has a heart for public health, healthcare, as a passion to serve, or a passion to learn. Connecting with those students who value me as a resource to take them to the next level is what energizes me.

Success is a feeling. Success is about the position of our hearts. Success means that we have all that we need and long for nothing. It does not mean we have it all. It does not mean we are perfect.

It means we have arrived at that place where we know that the Lord has blessed us and we have opened our hearts to whatever path He may have set before us. It is not a destination. Success is having the confidence and peace to enjoy the daily small victories and blessings. It is being able to sow into someone else's life even a small part of what we've been given.

I encourage ladies in academia to build your brand. *The Live Well* is a global wellness community I developed to support the wellness of women. It includes health coaching, wellness retreats, resources for women trying to conceive, live talks, and an online platform. My goal is to truly make wellness attainable for women throughout life's changes. Think about what brings you to work every day and what reflects your character, that's your brand.

The type of school you choose to teach in really will govern a large part of your experience. I encourage those entering academia to think about their needs and what type of school and classroom setting will meet those needs. While there are exceptions, understand that the public university experience and liberal arts university experiences will likely be night and day pertaining to classroom sizes and college priorities, and other factors.

Community colleges and commuter schools bring their own unique student profile regarding academic rigor, professional experience and even student attitudes toward education. Religious based schools allow faith in the classroom, but state schools will blast you for mentioning your own faith. Yes, there are exceptions. Online universities often have larger contingents of international students, which depending on your role, can cause challenges in scheduling meeting times or even understanding the language the student speaks.

There are also many benefits to each of these university models. It's really about finding the one that works for you, that you can accept the good and bad. It's like marriage. Or dating. You may have to try a few schools before you understand your own needs as a professor and the type of school that meets those needs, as well as where you can best contribute and are valued.

Two seasoned professors and two different universities—one state school, one HBCU—told me that teaching was like being on stage. As an introvert that presents as an extrovert, I could not have cringed more from that statement. I love being me. I connect best with students when they come to my office for one on one discussions about the public health issues that really matter to them. In the classroom, particularly in larger classes, connecting does have to come by way of entertainment. You have to be large enough for the student in the back of the lecture hall to still feel your energy. That can be draining for an introvert.

I best connect with students in the small classes. I love graduate classes. The grad students get into the critical analysis where I feel I can offer insight. They are past the stage of nickel and diming a professor for an "A" they did not earn. Whether you're an introvert or an extrovert, understanding your own communication style goes a long way toward maximizing the relationships you build with students. The best takeaway I have on connecting is to find something of value in the student. Find something they did well. Compliment their approach, their dedication, their kindness, or whatever makes them standout. We all standout for something, so (when they do) tell them.

I believe this is the exception, not the rule, but my performance was consistently evaluated by faculty members outside of my discipline. It became a challenge to align my approach with their expectations. As I considered whether or not to pursue tenure, as I was invited to transfer to the tenure track, I felt that it would be a losing battle at this particular institution. I was in a health department housed within a college of education, so there was already misalignment there. The faculty members evaluating performance came from kinesiology, not public health. There are very different approaches to research between the two disciplines, and they have different values as a whole. Gaining favorable consideration for tenure would have been a challenge.

My students all wanted to be elementary school teachers, and I had to climb the mountain of trying to get them excited about things like cancer stats and health outcomes. It was overall a poor match, and therefore also made for more instructional challenges that impacted my reviews based on classroom interactions and engagement. I encourage everyone to truly look at the position of your department within the college, the profile of faculty and whether or not there are enough faculty members from your discipline to form a core team, as well as the student profile to ensure that even at a basic level they will be engaged with the courses you will be assigned to teach.

Aside from doing your research ahead of time to ensure you are at the best kind of institution in the best fit department for you, I encourage you to stay diligent. Being promoted in academia, whether tenure-track or not, is a challenge. Researchers are a tough crowd. They are competitive and committed to their opinions. Find synergy with at least one other faculty member in your department, and a few faculty members across the school. This can support developing a solid interdisciplinary research portfolio, which yields publications, the currency of academia.

Now that I've been on the inside, I would have asked so many more questions during the faculty application process. It's important to remain gracious and not presumptuous in the interview, so asking the questions at the right time is imperative. There are answers I wish I would have had ahead of time to make a more educated decision about teaching at a state university that was also somewhat of a metropolitan area commuter school.

Some of the questions I would have asked include: How many classes do you assign a faculty member each term? Understanding whether I'm teaching two classes on the same topic, or two classes on different topics offers insight into the time I will have to spend prepping for one individual or two or more unique classes. This is the difference between preparing 15-weeks of lectures versus 45 weeks of lectures if I've been assigned three different courses. We all have a limit. For me, teaching more than two courses at a time stretches my brain too thin and I cannot focus or offer the best instruction. Teaching more than three classes per semester is too demanding of schedule, particularly given the commute I had. I had no research time allotted in my schedule, as a lecturer, I had no flexibility because all my classes were assigned to me.

Which brings me to some other questions: How much time can I spend on research? Does the department offer seed funding for research until my portfolio is built? Do faculty choose the courses they teach or are they assigned to them without input? Does faculty have the ability to structure their own teaching schedule or is that assigned by the department? Some larger-scale questions that are helpful are: What is the promotion progression here? Do others in this same role have the same level of education as I do? How is performance evaluated? How is tenure evaluated?

Luckily, I did not face many overt hurdles relating to gender. I believe faculty are smart enough now to at least cover up any biases they may have. Students are still practicing this art, so there are times when male students may try intimidation. They see it does not work, however, and then they back off. Managing those types of situations is a learned skill as well. I learned to place the power of the department on the student as soon as the instance would occur. I've had a 6-foot tall student hovering over me at 5'5" telling me I should do what he wants because his parents pay for this class. I would stand firmly, not back up, make eye contact, and slowly and calmly offer a meeting between the Chair, the student, and myself. Somehow, the meetings would never occur and their attitudes would change.

I was the first African-American women to serve on full-time faculty in my department. It was hard for me to grasp that some people had been at the university longer than I had been alive and had never worked directly with an African-American woman. Out of 100 applicants, the department chose me. I did not see overtly racist acts from faculty, but students often came with their own implicit biases about age, gender, and race, and were more overt about it. In the faculty setting, any of those attitudes were more at bay and may have played out by being ignored or receiving lower performance reviews for an undocumented reason.

Part-time online teaching has become my niche. I remain open to adjunct teaching on campus, but that is not for me right now with the time commitments of having young children. I get to engage in research when it works for me and leverage the research review team at my online institution, I have an academic affiliation to include in publication submissions, and the course load is flexible. Online teaching is its own culture, and you really have to find an institute that works for you in that regard as well. I carefully examined whether classes were synchronous or asynchronous and the classroom engagement requirements.

Not that I'm a biased co-editor of this book, but this *Black Woman's Guide* really is valuable in nailing down both the tangible and intangible factors that can make or break a career in academia. It shares valuable insights that are not widely known or public. I wish it was around when I first began considering academia. Other than that, I would have gotten a better idea of the promotion pathway before joining faculty and really take time to know faculty titles— the differences between senior lecturer, principal lecturer, lecturer, assistant, and associate professor, etc.—and where my education level truly fits in as compared to other faculty members who would have the same title.

I've had a challenge navigating non-traditional students who in many cases are older than me and are also leaders in the workplace. They are not always as teachable or coachable, so there can be some abrasive, even combative, exchanges there until they realize that their grade depends on soft skills like communication, respect, and following instruction.

To continue succeeding, take on the tasks you don't get paid for. Go above and beyond. Don't burn yourself out, but be known as the person who can get it done quickly and effectively. Dedication is revealed over time, so daily consistency is key. Relax from having to prove yourself. The calmness is refreshing in academia and will draw others toward you if you can maintain it.

For a long career in academia, design a lifestyle that works for you. You do not owe anyone an explanation for your career path or choices. Whether you teach online or in-person, each approach has its advantages and challenges. Pursuing a career in academia takes persistence and dedication. Understand your reasons for wanting to take this path. The prestige and image are not enough, but purpose and passion are. Then, just apply. Don't count yourself out. Start guest lecturing somewhere. Get into the adjunct pool at a community college so they can call you when they need you. Just start!

The Adjunct Experience

Karon L. Phillips, Ph.D., MPH, CHES, CAPS is a public health gerontologist working in the Washington, D.C. area. She's a scientific reviewer (contractor) for the NIH Center for Scientific Review and works as a community engagement consultant. She has significant experience conducting and coordinating a variety of coalition building and programmatic activities to promote healthy aging. Dr. Phillips has over 14 years of experience in applied gerontology and working with older adults from diverse backgrounds. She served as a health and aging policy fellow where she worked on Capitol Hill and at AARP. Dr. Phillips holds a Bachelor of Arts in English and Women's Studies from Cornell University. She received her Master of Public Health degree and her Doctorate in Aging Studies from the University of South Florida. She has spent seven years in academia.

Thoughts on advancing in academia from Dr. Phillips: I entered the field because I taught a class in graduate school and enjoyed it. I enjoyed sharing my knowledge about the field and the discussion with students. During my post-doc I applied to an online teaching position and started my adjunct journey.

I have held leadership in several positions with several professional organizations in gerontology and public health. I am currently serving on two professional boards. Also, I thoroughly enjoy mentoring emerging gerontologists and public health professionals. I feel like it is my responsibility to lift as I climb. I have learned a lot from my journey thus far and want to make sure that other people can be successful as well.

I'm inspired by healthy discussion in the class about a new topic, especially when the students bring up points without me prompting them and when they ask thought-provoking questions. I can then steer the discussion so that students are getting the most out of the class. I also enjoy seeing students that have taken one of my previous classes returning to be in my current class. It is flattering but reassuring that you are reaching them. Moreover, I get excited when I develop timely activities that the students benefit from. I make conscious efforts to create engaging activities that require the students to discuss, summarize, and present information.

For me, success is feeling whole. It is when you are accomplishing your individual goals and aspirations, and, in my opinion, setting an example for others.

For my online teaching position, I applied several places and finally landed one. It took some time and perseverance. For teaching at a traditional school, I was contacted by a colleague that knew my research interests and experiences. I shared my CV and excitement with her and she forwarded that on to the appropriate decision-makers. Later, I had a meeting with the faculty member that was over assigning people to the courses in the Fall and I was set up to teach a class that Spring semester. In this case, it was all in my network. Obtaining this position at a traditional university opened doors to other teaching opportunities.

I have experiences at public universities—with one focusing more on non-traditional and military students. I get the opportunity to teach a wide range of students at different phases in their lives. Some are young and hungry for information so they ask more probing questions. Then there are other students that may have worked in the particular field that we are discussing and they are able to add some additional context that we may not get from the texts. Both schools are a good fit for me because I teach and interact with all kinds of students, which I enjoy.

To be able to connect with students, you have to make the information applicable to the real world. In other words, find ways to connect the information back to experiences they will ultimately have in their future careers. I often make sure we discuss current events as well. The students are more engaged when we have these discussions and they can see how the information we are learning goes beyond theory.'

I have not encountered many hurdles, thankfully. From an adjunct perspective, I think the main challenge you have is the time it takes to get promoted as an adjunct, and if there is an opportunity for it. Thankfully there are adjunct committees that advocate for more support and opportunities. To overcome hurdles, you have to have resilience. Find out what you need to do to improve and keep moving forward. Give yourself some space to express any disappointments or setbacks, but do not dwell in that space for too long. Keep moving.

Many applicants would like to know more about the promotion potential for adjunct faculty to full-time faculty. Inquire about if and how people make the transition from adjunct to full-time faculty at that particular institution. I do not think gender has impacted my teaching experience. However, my race has enriched my experience. Some students have shared with me that I am the first African American professor that they have had. That has always motivated me to be a positive example to them. I do think being a younger African American adjunct professor you do have some students that will test the waters with you. Some students assume you do not care and may not be as invested as their full-time professors. I have had a few occasions where students thought I was a pushover (for lack of better terms) but I dot my I's and cross my T's. I support all my students but they do have to be honest and do the work.

My mother always told me as a child "You make time." I did not understand what that meant until I got much older. I check in with myself often. I keep a pretty full calendar (working full-time, part-time teaching, and consulting) and I am very active in Batala Washington (an Afro-Brazilian drumming group). Plus I enjoy traveling, swimming, reading, and creating tablescapes. But I make sure I take care of myself and schedule self-care time. Taking care of myself includes those core components that keep me going. For example, I have to meal prep and have a general idea of what I am wearing for the week on Sunday. I enjoy cooking (I call my kitchen my lab) so that was never the challenge, but I would not always pack up my lunches ahead of time to take with me. I would delay and plan to do it in the mornings but would run out of time because I was throwing clothes around trying to decide what I am going to wear. I now pack up my breakfast and lunch for the week ahead of time. As far as work clothes, I have basically invested in building up my wardrobe so that I would not have to spend much time on this endeavor every morning. In the past, I spent a lot of time pulling out clothes trying to figure out my outfit. I was then left with an outfit that I was not always satisfied with and a pile of clothes that I generally did not want to hang back up after the day was over.

In sum, taking care of myself is more about knowing myself and making sure I have measures in place to support me. Self-care, for me, can be the stereotypical baths, aromatherapy, vacations, etc., but it can also be unplugging from my computer and cell phone, making sure I spend time with friends, taking my dog for a walk, or just sitting down with a cup of tea on my balcony and breathing. Drumming is also a form of self-care for me in that I get some exercise and support from the women in my drumming group. I also try to learn at least two new things a year. Last year it was cake decorating and learning sign language. Lastly, I track my schedule via a traditional planner and electronically, and I make sure there is time for myself. I think I like both because I can decorate the traditional planner with stickers and motivational quotes. I like using my e-calendar for setting reminders. Overall, self-care is all about knowing your limitations and when you need to rest, reflect, and restore.

I feel like I learn something every day that I wish I knew years ago. We learn things from great mentors, unsupportive bosses, seeing other people fumble, seeing something you worked on not work out at all, positive feedback, awards, unhealthy work environments, great colleagues and friends, general life successes, and unexpected tests. I could list more but overall, we learn from everything we experience in life. Each step that I take in my career, I apply what

I know went well in the past and what did not go as planned to the next opportunity. One overarching thing I can say that it is important is to do your research for every opportunity. Do not just take it because it is there. Consider if it is right for you and if it will help you move forward.

Overall, my biggest lesson learned over the years is an understanding—no matter who you are, where you are in life, and what your intentions are... there will be people that will try consistently to prevent you from achieving your goals. It has nothing to do with you. I could tell quite a few stories but I have learned how to channel that which I initially found confusing, disappointing, and frustrating to my growth, building myself up, and strengthening myself. I am sure I will encounter these people and situations again and again, but I take something from each experience. So, because of these experiences, I vowed to always empower people, especially my sisters. I have been in spaces where my sisters in the academy, unfortunately, were not supportive, to say the least, and I do not want that cycle to continue.

Working in three areas that I am passionate about has been my greatest success so far. I have always enjoyed research and science and my current full-time position allows me to support some of the leading efforts to advance health. Working with aging seniors in my community to help them connect with innovative programs is a lot of fun to me. I enjoy teaching because I enjoy sharing my knowledge of the field and empowering future leaders.

Teaching is rewarding but it takes a lot of commitment. Make sure you are ready for the time and energy that it takes to be successful in your role. For those interested in adjunct teaching, start by writing a good cover letter highlighting your experience teaching and/or giving presentations. Again, highlight how your expertise will translate to the classroom. I recommend working with a professional resume editor so that they can pull out your expertise that connects well with teaching. If you do not have experience teaching or giving presentations, then volunteer! I often asked friends to come in to give guest lectures. Find a way to give community presentations on a topic of interest to you.

Also, start networking! Network to stand out. I also think you have to establish a professional brand for yourself. Basically connecting your name with a specific area of expertise so that when people think about that area they immediately think about you. The same networking rules you used to get your full-time job applies in the adjunct setting as well. If you have a colleague that is a full-time professor at a university you are interested in, talk to them. They have more contact with the decision-makers in the department. Sometimes adjuncts can help get your name in front of the right people, but keep in mind that adjuncts do not always have a lot of contact with their home department and they are in large pools to get selected for classes. Also, keep applying. I applied to one school several times over the course of several years before I was hired.

The HBCU Perspective

Kesha Baptiste-Roberts, Ph.D., MPH is an assistant professor in the Department of Public Health Analysis at Morgan State University, School of Community Health and Policy. Dr. Baptiste-Roberts has published research in the areas of maternal and child health, women's health, type 2 diabetes and obesity. Her early work was primarily focused on pregnancy-related factors and their influence on chronic diseases specifically diabetes and obesity across the life course. Her current research efforts are focused on health among sexual minority women. Dr. Baptiste-Roberts has a wealth of teaching experience and has taught introductory and advanced level epidemiology and subject-specific courses such as maternal child health epidemiology and social epidemiology. She is an active member of the Epidemiology Section of the American Public

Health Association (APHA) and has served in several leadership roles. She is also the president of the Society of the Analysis of African American Public Health Issues (SAAPHI). Dr. Baptiste-Roberts currently serves as an assistant professor at two academic institutions.

Thoughts from advancing in academia from Dr. Baptiste-Roberts: I enjoy being in an environment where there is time and space for the discussion of innovative ideas and concepts. I get paid to dive deeply in the topics of interest, to think and learn! The flexibility of academia appealed to me. I work independently, and I can structure my time in a way the best suits me. Although academia allows for independent work, you collaborate and are mentored by others, so you are not alone. Academia also allows for teaching and making an impact on the public health workforce of the future. I like the idea of having a hand in inspiring young people to be their best and training them for the challenges of the future.

I serve on the leadership team of the Epidemiology Section of the American Public Health Association (APHA). I currently serve as a section councilor and co-chair of Scientific Programs for the Epidemiology Section. In the past, I served two terms on the Governing Council as well. In addition, I am serving my last term as the president of the Society for the Analysis of African American Public Health Issues [SAAPHI]. Prior to becoming president, I served as the chair of the Scientific Committee. I also serve as an executive member of the SANKOFA, collective. The SANKOFA Collaborative is a national partnership of African American and Afro-Latino health professionals dedicated to addressing the impact of HIV/AIDS on African American women and their families. This group was established during the planning and execution of the "Paradigm Shift: The Impact of HIV/AIDS on African American Women & Families" conference in Atlanta, 2017. I am also an active member of the American College of Epidemiology and the Society for Epidemiologic Research. Every year I volunteer to review abstracts. I also serve the field by serving as a reviewer for various journals. I've also served as a grant reviewer for the Health Resources and Services Administration Maternal and Child Health Block grants.

I am energized as a professor because I feel a sense of urgency to train public health professionals to combat the persisting and in some cases increasing disparities in health. We need representation in the public health workforce from disadvantaged communities and minority groups who are well trained and can build the bridge between the public health officials and systems and the community. I am always energized after research brainstorming sessions or research question refinement discussions with doctoral students. Success to me is following your own path, fulfilling your purpose, working hard to be the best you can be and uplifting others to be their best. After my Ph.D. and postdoctoral fellowship, I took an academic job as an assistant professor.

I am currently at an HBCU after being at a predominantly white institution [PWI]. I completed all my tertiary education at PWIs. My passion for eliminating health disparities and achieving health equity makes my current position an excellent choice for me. Often, the decision-makers and persons of power controlling the money are not members of the disadvantaged groups or the groups experiencing the effects of discriminatory policies and practices. I am passionate about empowering members of disadvantaged groups and groups that have been subject to discriminatory policies that have adversely affected the health and wellbeing of their communities with the knowledge and skills to effectively advocate for the promotion of health and well-being of their communities.

It is not enough for folks to have a seat at the table, but when they are afforded a seat at the table they need to be effective. At an HBCU, the approach to education is more holistic. There is a family atmosphere that is absent at PWIs. However, the HBCU also has its challenges. These institutions are often under-resourced and lack efficient administration systems and processes. The students in the program within which I teach are mostly employed full time and so I've had to utilize innovative teaching strategies that are efficient and amenable to the commuter and the adult learner.

Invest time in getting to know your students at the beginning of the semester and give them the opportunity to get to know you. Although some may think that an icebreaker is a waste of time, I've found that it has been extremely helpful and it has guided the assembling of groups and activities. It is important to decrease the distance between the podium and the students so that students are comfortable asking questions, seeking clarification, expressing frustration with difficult concepts or simply asking you to explain the concept in a different way.

Some of the challenges I have faced are that the criteria on which the performance evaluation was based was not communicated to me and there were no written criteria, which were hurdles I have encountered. I would suggest strongly having a mentor with whom you can have frank discussions regarding the process and requirements for promotion and tenure. There are some essential resources that I would highly recommend for new minority faculty members so that you use your time efficiently and avoid pitfalls that derail new faculty. Even when systems or processes do not exist at your institution, you need to be creative so that you ensure documentation of your activities. You may need to initiate a performance evaluation for yourself, provide the forms and essentially create the process so that you will have what you need for your dossier and to be successful.

I wish I had asked for more specifics regarding administrative support in general as well as grant writing support and grant administration. In addition, I wish I had asked a bit more about the vision for the school/program. Then I would have been able to assess my fit with respect to the direction of the school/program. Gender *has* impacted my faculty experience, but I do not think that this is unique to academia. The weight of family responsibilities has traditionally fallen more on the female. As such, it continues to be a challenge to balance family and work. However, given that public health is a female-dominated field and the academic leadership at the school level at my institution is female-dominated, I believe that my experience has been fair.

At my first academic job, I believe that race did affect my faculty experience. I felt that the school administration was happy to have a minority faculty as this would demonstrate some diversity. However, I also felt pigeonholed into automatically being on the diversity committee. I felt at times I was unnecessarily being challenged and questioned. Given comments in meetings about minority student applicants, there seemed to be this belief that minority students were not up to par with white students and there needed to be some concessions made for them. This was quite disturbing to me and explained why I was being constantly challenged.

This remains a challenge. It is rare that there is a perfect balance. This is constantly a work in progress. I do a Sunday night planning activity where I review my yearly goals, monthly goals and set weekly goals. I plan activities for the week to work toward achieving those weekly goals. Sometimes, my goals are unrealistic and other times they are realistic. There are times when everything falls into place and sometimes when life just happens, and I have to make adjustments.

I tend to not live with regrets. At times, I wish I had stayed a little bit longer at the institution where I trained and launched my career before moving on to another place. Sometimes, I wish that I didn't accept my first academic position since it was not a good fit in so many ways. However, this job also provided me with an amazing experience with my first doctoral student, who graduated under my guidance. I think that I would have advocated for myself a bit more and sought out the support of my mentors earlier in my first academic job.

It is important to spend the time to assess what's going on in your field, have discussions with your peers, and think about new and innovative approaches. The time spent reading and thinking is invaluable.

Balance of family and career has been the biggest challenge for me thus far. However, despite the demands of family and personal commitments, I have been able to produce. Academia is tough, but it is exciting and rewarding. It's easy to get lost, but with good planning, mentorship, support, and hard work, the sky is the limit. The core piece of advice is to be well prepared and well organized. It is important to establish healthy mentorship relationships and supportive relationships with your peers, set realistic goals, and actively work toward those goals.

From Military to Teaching Online

Dr. Sandra M. Harris, Ph.D. holds a Doctor of Philosophy in Educational Psychology as well as a Master's of Education in School Psychometry from Auburn University in Alabama. She obtained her Master of Arts and Bachelor Arts degrees in Psychology from California State University. Dr. Harris' professional background includes 20 years of active duty service in the United States Air Force. During those twenty years, she gained experience in areas such as avionics communication, aircraft maintenance, strategic planning, quality improvement, leadership, management, supervision, supply functions, and career counseling.

Thoughts on advancing in academia from Dr. Harris: My current position is assessment director in the College of Social and

Behavioral Sciences at Walden University. I have been at Walden, an accredited online institution, for nearly thirteen years. I came to Walden after leaving a traditional brick and mortar institution that I had been affiliated with for over fifteen years. I began with Walden as a contributing faculty member during October 2005 in the School of Psychology. I became a core faculty on January 1, 2010. My current affiliation is primarily with the Ph.D. Human Services program. However, I serve on dissertation committees in several other programs as well.

I have been working with adult learners in higher education for approximately twenty-eight years. My entry into academia was rather serendipitous. This career trajectory is not one I sought during my early years, nor was it something I had thought I was particularly well suited for. My trajectory began during my military career. I served twenty years in the United States Air Force. I was originally trained as an avionics communications technician, a specialty which was 97% male at the time I entered the field. After serving in the avionics career field for several years and becoming increasingly frustrated with what was being required of avionics technicians, I decided it was time to make a career change. The only field that I felt remotely attracted to was professional military education (PME). I submitted the paperwork to cross-train and was accepted. It was in the military that I received formal training on how to be an instructor. The training consisted of 4 weeks of Academic Instructor School where I was taught the technical aspects of teaching. I was exposed to processes such as curriculum development, developing a syllabus, developing learning outcomes, developing learning outcomes, test item construction, test items analysis, and different aspects of teaching such as the use of case studies, guided discussions, use of lectures and experiential learning, etc.

My first assignment as a PME instructor at the Noncommissioned Officer Academy: The first few weeks were a bit painful as the actual act of teaching was much different in practice than it was in theory. After 3 weeks of stage fright and 8 pounds of weight loss, I found my stride in teaching after having a long discussion with a colleague who informed me that learning is a two-way street. The colleague informed me that as in instructor, the best I could do would be to be prepared for the lectures and to give my best effort with each block of instruction. She stated that it would be ultimately up to the students to learn the material or not. Those words of wisdom went a long way toward shaping my trajectory in academia. The words moved me into a mental space of confidence, which translated into my teaching. It was shortly after the conversation with my colleague that I knew I had found my calling and that I wanted to further pursue academia after I retired from the military. At that point, I still had 8 years until I reached the twenty-year mark.

It has been 21 years since I retired, and my trajectory into the virtual environment also marked a turning point which I had not anticipated. I have been employed full time in the virtual academy for about 8 years. I have been teaching in the virtual environment for approximately sixteen years. I was introduced to the virtual environment by another colleague who had a vision. He wanted to offer online classes to nontraditional students whose work schedules made it difficult for them to attend traditional classes. He asked if I would develop and teach a couple of introductory psychology courses. He knew of my background in curriculum development, and I said sure. Little did I know that the request would ultimately lead to full-time employment in the virtual work world. The same colleague who asked me to develop the online courses also introduced me to Walden University. He sent me an email regarding a position announcement for contributing faculty. I sent an email expressing my interest in teaching along with my curriculum vitae. I was hired by sending just the one email.

During my career in academia, I have held titles such as director, department chair, and I currently hold the title of assessment director. I serve the field through service and engagement inside of the university where I am employed as well as with several professional organizations outside of the university. I serve several committees at the university and as a reviewer for several journals. I also serve as methodology advisor and mentor for organizations that are dedicated to promoting the success and advancement of women, particularly women of color, in the academy.

The thing that inspires me most as a professor is witnessing the success of individuals whom I mentor. The first note of inspiration is witnessing individuals who come from very challenging backgrounds complete their doctoral degrees. I am thinking of three individuals who defied the labels placed upon them as children and were labeled uneducable. Each individual had some form of cognitive impairment which impacted the rate at which they acquired information. One person was dyslexic, one person experienced a traumatic brain injury, and the third had a reading disability...yet all displayed dedication, determination, and persistence in completing their doctoral degree. Neither of the three revealed their past educational challenges until the day of the final dissertation defense. Each thanked the committee for supporting and guiding their journey to the Ph.D. In several other cases, I had the privilege of being on the committees of individuals who were formerly children of foster care, yet they persisted to earn their PhDs. There are many other stories...but the stories of the individuals referenced here and their success have inspired and motivated me to continue mentoring others who pursue a doctoral degree.

I define success as a person achieving a goal or task that he or she set about to accomplish. Success is very much an individual journey. What is success for one may or may not be success for others. I also do not believe that success has an end state, meaning success is fluid. Individuals can be successful in many ways while pursuing the same endeavor. I encourage individuals to determine what success is for them and to subsequently develops goals, strategies, and milestones to achieve that success.

The program which I am mostly affiliated with is a good fit for me as a professor because a large percentage of the students are Brown men and women. When I attend the various functions such as residencies and dissertation intensives, students will frequently comment on how few people of color they encounter at the residences and intensives. Many have said that I was the first person of color they had seen in residencies. I am cognizant that for many students I serve as a visual model of the success they are striving to attain by earning the Ph.D. This knowledge brings some pressure as I occasionally feel as though I am the fishbowl and everyone is watching. I feel compelled to be professional at all times. Occasionally, I feel the pull to be the perfect image of the professional Brown woman in academia. At times that pull becomes overwhelming and personally taxing as I sometimes overextend myself in the service of others, which can negatively impact my work-life balance. I came to accept my position as a role model many years ago. In doing so I have become acutely aware that the success I have attained does cast me as a model whose behavior others strive to emulate. It is a position that I take seriously and my position in the program where I am affiliated is a good fit and a good choice for me because I can mentor other Brown women as they work to become a part of academia.

My advice for connecting with students is to make one's self available to have conversations with them. I am available to chat with students as frequently as the students would like to chat. I speak with some students by phone weekly. Others I communicate with via email. Others prefer to text, and a few prefer to connect through Skype or other electronic mediums. Ultimately though, students must want to make the connection. Though I communicate frequently with most students, there are others whom I rarely hear from, and that is okay. I let those students know that I am available. I personally have not encountered issues with performance evaluations while in academia. I have consistently received ratings that I have earned. I also have not personally encountered hurdles with promotion considerations. When serving at the former brick and mortar institution I received a promotion and tenure on the first submission. I actually walked away from a full professorship. The former university went through several administrative and structural changes, which changed the work environment from one of joy and fulfillment to one of dread and disdain. The last dean whom I served under came into the position with no experience in academia. The decisions and approaches the dean took toward students and faculty served to undermine the authority of faculty in the course room. The environment became noncollegial and toxic. All trust and respect were lost. I came to dread going into the office at the start of each week because I feared the ineffective changes. At the point where I became completely disillusioned and my job satisfaction hit its lowest point, I had already submitted an application for full professor. It was also about this point where the core position in assessment was advertised at Walden University. I applied for the position at Walden and was later made an offer. I accepted the offer and submitted my letter of resignation on the same day. I did not hear about the promotion to full professor until after I had made the decision to leave that institution. In retrospect, I am not sure I would have stayed at the institution even if I had gotten notice of promotion to full professor before tendering my resignation. I only know that after I made up my mind to leave the institution, I was not turning back. I say all of this to emphasize that there is more to job satisfaction than just promotion. I could not see staying in a job to receive a promotion while being dissatisfied and disgruntled.

The first step to overcoming hurdles to promotion is to know what is required to be promoted. This means knowing about the formal written rules for promotion and going the step further to inquire about the unwritten rules for the promotion. Gaining access to the faculty guide will provide easy access to formal, written rules. Gaining information about informal rules will be a bit more challenging. Becoming familiar with informal rules for promotion will require some socialization and networking with individuals who have gone through the process as well as establishing connections with individuals who may have served on promotion and tenure committees. Individuals who enter academia should start working to meet the requirements for promotion from the day they step foot on the campus, be that campus virtual or on the ground.

One cannot spend the last 2 years of a 5-year promotion cycle to start preparing for a promotion or tenure. One must demonstrate the intent to earn promotion and record performance across time. For women, as well as other Black and Brown people in academia, it is imperative to understand that meeting the minimum requirements for promotion may not be enough for people of color. Expect to work harder than colleagues of European ancestry to achieve promotion and tenure. Excel at a rate that is slightly higher than those peers.

Before I moved into academia full-time I was an adjunct professor. At the second university where I worked there was an older gentleman who took it upon himself to mentor me in the rules and unwritten rules of academia. I am not sure of why, but he decided the second time he saw me that he wanted to be my mentor. I recall being in the faculty office one day copying exams for a course I was teaching. He came into office and introduced himself. Stated he had heard there was a new faculty on campus and stated that he had assumed that I was the new faculty person. He seemed to know a lot more about me than I knew of him. At the time he stated he was also aware that I was on active duty. He shared his story about being on active duty and how he entered academia. He then asked if teaching was something I planned to do after I retired. To which I replied, "Yes I have given it some thought."

He then invited me to come by and chat with him when I had the time. He said he wanted to offer some insight and suggestions on what I needed to ask or inquire about when I decided to become a full-time faculty if I planned to stay at the university. I took him up on his offer. Little did I know just how valuable his chat sessions would be. When I was offered a teaching position at the university I was able to negotiate and obtain a lot of things based on our earlier conversations. This individual also provided me with a great deal of information about retirement and what to do to start planning for retirement.

I do not feel that my gender or my race have had an impact on my faculty experience. I think my twenty years of military experience and my experience with teaching shaped my professional demeanor and having worked in a previously male-dominated career field resulted in me developing a sort of "persona" (in a sense) that transcended stereotypical notions of race and gender. Now, gender and my military experience is a whole different story and a totally different book chapter. I experienced a great deal of opposition and backlash while pursuing my education when I was still in uniform. So, by the time I retired I was over the gender bias as it related to women pursuing advanced degrees.

However, I am cognizant that gender equity issues do exist in academia. I am aware that although women obtain doctoral degrees at the same rate, or slightly higher than males, there are still gender disparities in terms of pay and career advancement. All factors being equal, women still earn lower pay and advance at a slower pace than their male counterparts. Moreover, Brown women face further disparities because of our skin color. These disparities are why I am affiliated with organizations which work to promote the career advancement of women in academia. Being affiliated with these organizations enables me to connect with and mentor others in the processes associated with negotiating appropriately for resources according to their worth and not their gender or skin color.

Although I have retired twice over, maintaining work-life balance is an area which still requires conscious thought and planning. Achieving work-life balance in the virtual academy is a greater issue than I thought it would be. Because I work from home, my family has different expectations of me and my time. They do not realize that I actually DO WORK from home. They expect that I have the flexibility to be their personal assistant who can take care of their needs and wishes at any time of day. They expect that I can just hop in the car and bring them items which they left on the way to either school or work. I get calls sometimes asking, "What are you doing." When I say I am working, they respond, "Oh really." After 8 years of working from home, one would think that the question would have been put to rest by now.

I also have difficulty achieving work-life balance because it is hard sometimes to unplug from the virtual work world. I find myself checking emails well beyond the end of the workday. I check emails on weekends and even on vacation at times. The students whom I mentor frequently expect me to be available at their convenience. The majority of them work full-time jobs and can only work on assignments after work or on the weekend. And while I understand that, I have to set parameters about when I will be available because I have found myself logging 14 hour days 6 to 7 days a week, which leads to mental exhaustion. I want to be there for the students, but I have come to realize that having an adequate work-life balance is important for a person's mental health and overall job satisfaction. It was much easier to establish that work-life balance when I worked at a traditional brick and mortar campus. Basically, I was not on campus during the days when I did not teach classes. The administration did not expect me to be there, and students did not expect me to be available on days when I did not teach classes.

To achieve work-life balance, I have come to set specific times where I will be available to my students. I do make exceptions for special cases such as scheduling oral defense calls. I publish announcements and send emails to inform my students of when I will be available to them. Prior to setting those boundaries students felt free to call or contact me at any hour. I have received calls at 2.00 AM, 5:00 AM, and all of the hours in between. I received such calls on the weekend too. Establishing it and communication reduced the range of inappropriate calls. To achieve balance with regard to research and services, I have established specific days and times for which I will engage in each. Having a schedule of times and dates enables me to achieve a more manageable work-life balance.

I am happy with my trajectory and accomplishments thus far. I have met some amazing, wonderful people on this journey. Many of those people have become long-time friends. Many of those people I have not communicated with for years. There are special people who have had a lasting impact in ways I had never anticipated. If I had done things differently I probably would not have had the privilege and opportunity to have made contact with those amazing people.

Have a passion and care for whatever work you choose to engage in. When we have a passion for something, that passion will be evident to others. The passion will emanate in our eyes, voice, and very being when we talk to others about that work. Without passion and care, it will be difficult to stand out. Without passion doing the work will become tedious and unfulfilling, and that negative affect will also show when communicating with others.

One must disseminate one's work as broadly as possible through professional and community audiences. Attend and present your work at professional conferences. You can do poster sessions as well as give oral presentations at professional and community conferences. Publish your work in peer-reviewed journals and publications. Write about your work in book chapters. Become an editor or reviewer for a journal and share your work with other editors where possible. Share your work with all who will listen.

I have been fortunate since I have not experienced any challenges in academia. Again, I think this is partly due to my having entered academe in my late 30s after spending twenty years in the Air Force. I grew and matured in the military. I developed effective leadership, communication, conflict resolutions strategies, and management skills that were easily transferred to the academic setting. I entered academia with a degree of wisdom and insight that has enabled me to negotiate with others when needed.

My biggest success was receiving the promotion to full professor in the minimum required time and on the first submission. I was not present during the promotion committee meeting, but I was informed that there were several people who advocated strongly on my behalf. Ultimately, the decision was made because I met and exceeded all stipulated requirements for the promotion. I worked diligently to complete the specified, written requirements for a promotion. I also made an effort to talk to individuals who had been through the promotion process and who received a promotion to full professor. I talked to individuals who had applied for full professor and had been denied the promotion. I learned from each of those individuals and applied what I learned when it was time to submit my application.

My main piece of advice for a Brown woman seeking to enter or advance in academia is to connect with a mentor in academia. I actually suggest having several mentors. Establish connections with others who have been in academia and know the ropes, so to speak. In those connections, connect with people who can serve as mentors and sponsors, and be sure to understand the difference and need for each. Mentors are role models who can be instrumental in socializing Brown women into a community of scholars in the community. Mentors can be helpful in terms of communicating the challenges that Brown women face in academia, and mentors can be instrumental in helping Brown women develop strategies for overcoming those challenges and barriers. Mentors are individuals who take interest in both one's personal and professional development.

On the other hand, the sponsor is one who is in a position to provide opportunities for advancement. The sponsor is one who provides access to people and resources that can lead to professional growth and development. However, the sponsor may or may not take the time to provide the guidance and encouragement that typically comes from mentors. Occasionally, some women become lucky and have the privilege of having a mentor/sponsor in the same person. But this is not the norm. Therefore, it is important to know the role, need, and importance of having a mentor and a sponsor in academia. It is important to know the value of such individuals when it comes to achieving success in academia.

Work-Life Integration

Dr. Ford serves as a core faculty member, MS Counseling, School of Counseling at Walden University and has experienced seventeen years in academia. Including serving as adjunct faculty and assistant professor.

Thoughts on advancing in academia from Dr. Ford: My doctoral studies prepared me to provide clinical assessments, mental health counseling, supervision and to serve as a faculty/professor in graduate education programs. Through my academic occupational experiences, I have been privileged to serves as a staff member, professor, and administrator (school of counseling and university leadership). Initially, my focus was on being a psychologist. While completing my doctoral-level internship I was supervised and mentored by Dr. Paula Britton. While being supervised on clinical counseling, graduate teaching philosophies, and supervision I began to become aware of the privileges and rights of being a member of academia. Dr. Britton demonstrated how a professor facilitated the learning process, aiding graduate students with personal and professional development, engaged in research while being mindful of civic duties and social justice activities in academia and the community.

In addition to serving in academia, I serve inside and outside of my university. Over the years, I have been involved in a working group to gain accreditation for academic programs and the reaccreditation of the university. For the Council for the Accreditation of Education Programs (CACREP) School of Counseling program accreditations, I have written and edited accreditation standard replies, organized faculty, students and site supervisors to participate in the accreditation process. While serving as a member of a working group for the reaccreditation of the university I wrote parts of the university's reply to the accreditation standards, served as a member of the university social change activities and participated in site visit interviews.

I have served on thesis and dissertation committees as well as being the chairperson. Currently, I serve as a diversity and inclusion ambassador (DIA) for my institution and national faculty meeting ambassador (NFMA). Being an inaugural member of DIA allows me to support diversity and inclusion initiatives by supporting faculty, providing recommendations for university policies and curriculum development. It is a privilege to be a part of this initiative and look forward to enhancing our institution. As an NFMA, I support new faculty by assisting individuals with understanding how to prepare for the meeting and commencement prior to the event, connecting with my new colleague on-site to respond to any new questions while serving as a support person and if help is needed during our meetings and/or commencement.

I am active in my faith community as well. I serve on the Women's

Ministry Team where I apply my knowledge and skill to programs, strategic planning, and additional ministry activities. I have served on a local hospital, patient, and family advisory committee. I've been a member (and currently hold memberships) in the following professional organizations: American Counseling Association, Association for Counselor Education and Supervision, Ohio Counseling Association, Association for Humanistic Counseling and the American Psychological Association.

Currently, I am on the membership committee for my state counseling association. In my local community, I present to various organizations in the community on the topic of mental health, depression, healthy relationships, occupation conversations with local high school students, etc. In 2017 I was excited to launch the inaugural Mental Health Awareness Month at a local megachurch. The month-long activities included weekly public service announcements (print media, video during Sunday services, and on the websites). A one-day conference with a keynote speaker, videos on peoples' experiences with mental health concerns, and breakout sessions. There was a program for adolescents and for the parents of children (infants to late childhood). Also, information on child development was provided along with additional resources if needed. This initiative continues to serve people and is now offered yearly.

Currently, I am inspired by the ability to enrich the lives of others. Whether it be a local community outreach program, a speaking engagement, or through teaching and mentoring in academia. I am zealous for assisting others. Early in life, I learned giving people my best when I engage them for ten minutes or four hours assists people with feeling as if someone cares and is supportive of them. I enjoy encouraging others. I believe those who have been encouraged should encourage others. I enjoy being a part of academia because it provides me the opportunity to assist others in an academic setting and engage members of my community. It is a great balance for me since I can instruct, engage in research, and serve the people of my community. I am inspired by supporting others with the obtainment of their goals and continuing one's professional pursuits when one is faced with challenges.

For me, success continues to change during different seasons of my life. Initially, success was defined by academic pursuits. Once I entered the profession I was eager to engage in new activities (i.e. learning pedagogy, skills for teaching online, development of academic programs, and developing expertise for counseling and clinical psychology). As I become older I am still excited by these activities but I have also defined success by being available to my family and friends. My personal development has been salient for me and this is a part of my success story (I am looking forward to learning what future chapters will hold).

Entering academia was a natural fit for me. As I shared earlier, I obtained a degree in counselor education and supervision. A primary focus on my training was on graduate teaching, supervision, and leadership. I worked closely with my supervisor during field experience and gained insight into academic leadership, program development, mentoring student, and research.

Serving at an online university with hybrid teaching models (i.e. online, use of videoconference technology and face to face training (i.e. residencies/pre-practicum) was a good choice for me because I have always been intrigued by new endeavors and the development of new programs, schools, as well as initiatives. When I became employed by an online institution it was a new method of instruction and was not as common as it is today. In addition to online education being a new endeavor when I began teaching at my current university, I was also excited about the opportunity for people to obtain graduate degrees that may not have been accepted to a traditional graduate program. I was excited about the broad access mission and being able to aid students with obtaining their degree and the trajectory of their lives (this is one way I define success). In addition, the positive social change efforts at my institution allow people to apply what is learned in the classroom to enhance their communities and populations of interest.

Videoconferences allow me to see and hear students. I employ cultural humility strategies so I can become aware of the students' experiences in the classroom and outside of the classroom. Since I teach online, I am pleased to see and hear my students. It has been my experience that students feel the same and enjoy the ability to connect with faculty outside of the classroom. For my students who experience great difficulty, I offer to meet with them regularly throughout the quarter. I connect with students during conferences and during professional meetings. I look forward to having former students as colleagues and watching individuals have a great impact on their communities.

Remember to continue to pursue your dreams. I work on one task at a time to reach goals. Physical fitness and healthy eating aid me with being equipped to address hurdles in academia.

I have been promoted and experienced challenges with support. I became a member of a professional support community, called Affinity Group to discuss success, challenges, and future pursuits. The Affinity Group is comprised of African American women who serve as faculty and academic leaders at my university. In addition to the Affinity Group, I have other groups of professional women who are younger, older and work in various disciplines to process my experience and to share ideas as well as the development of collaborative efforts to help with achieving our professional and personal goals.

I recommend requesting and/or making opportunities to connect with individuals who are full professors and serve in various roles in the institution. I also recommend learning and understand the culture of the work environment while networking with members of the institution (engaging in service across the university is a great way to meet colleges in and outside of your college).

Immediately after I completed my doctoral program I interviewed for an MS Counseling assistant professor position. While participating in the interview process I was scheduled to meet with the provost of the university. The provost (a man of color) informed me, I would never have difficulty securing a job in the academy because I am two-four. I did not know what this meant, so I sought clarification. He responded you are African American and a woman; therefore, you are a two for one since higher education institutions need to diversify. I was astonished and this was my first introduction to perceptions of race and sex in the academy for employees. I understood the challenges as a student but not as an employee. I was upset because I began to feel like I felt several times as a doctoral student when my peers would discuss diversity and one person shared the perspective that people of color were enrolled in the program due to affirmative action.

I decided I did not want to be perceived as a quota filler in my graduate program (I excelled and was the first one to defend my dissertation and graduate). I knew and still know that God gives me wisdom, knowledge, and understanding. He will direct my path no matter what others think or say. Regardless of perceptions of gender and race, I can do all things through Christ that strengthen me.

The prior example illustrates my introduction to race and sex in academia. My work in academia has been with international students and site supervisors. As an African American, I am open to discussing race and ethnic considerations (from experiences in my community of origin and professional training) and from my experiences as a graduate student and employee. Due to my experiences I have learned to listen to others, to take the risk (yes, it can be a risk), to engage in conversations with my colleagues and leadership team on race, my experiences, perceptions of interactions, and my responses to our interactions to make my work community a safe and respectful place for all. When doing so there have been moments when I had to apologize and learn from others related to diversity in academia.

To support faculty of color, I have presented on recruitment and retention for diverse faculty, I became a member of the inaugural class of diversity and inclusion ambassador for my university to aid with improvements for students, faculty, staff, and the curriculum. I use cultural humility strategies, self-reflection, and process my experiences regarding race and diversity and engage my colleagues to create a supportive learning community for all.

This has not been easy tasks since I care for an ill mother and am rearing children. I had to prioritize my family and know I will have opportunities to engage in teaching, research, and other professional goals. I have found collaborating with my colleagues is a beneficial way to engage in the duties of academia while fulfilling my personal commitments.

Next time around, I'd maintain better contact with some of the people I have met at conferences and worked. I am pleased professional networks and social media resources provide opportunities to engage with more people I meet outside of my workplace. For those interested in the advancement, keep working on all of your areas of interest. Volunteer and try new professional development opportunities because you never know where an opportunity may become available. Continue to collaborate with colleagues, staff, and members of my community.

My biggest challenge has been being terminated from a position without probable cause. Even with this situation, there have been far greater successes. Being the first member of my family to obtain a Ph.D. and helping other family members achieve their academic goals. My biggest success as a member of academia is being a member of a talented team that developed accredited graduate programs and resulted in the creation of the School of Counseling at an accredited university.

For those on the academic path, keep going. No matter what happens and the obstacles one may face, keep working toward the goal because there is much more to pursuit. I am excited to learn what the future will hold because I know it is going to be great! Obstacles may enter your path. Do. Not. Quit. If you take a break due to frustration do not delay for too long. Get up, journal, talk with your support system and keep going. Being flexible is important. Be open to hear and learn different ideas and perspectives. Be a person of integrity. Do the right thing even when no one is watching. Conscientiousness is key. Acknowledge the contributions of others. Elevate others; it is wonderful to support your colleagues and contribute to their success.

Master's Degree and Many Hats

Terri Floyd, MS a Little Rock native, wears many hats. She is a proud mother, IT business analyst, entrepreneur, philanthropist, and adjunct professor, to name a few. She's a graduate of Philander Smith College with a Bachelor of Arts degree in Psychology, University of Arkansas Little Rock with a Pos-Graduate certificate in Gerontology (aging studies) and a Master of Science degree in Health Sciences with an emphasis in Health Education and Health Promotion.

She has extensive years of working experience in education, mental health, public health, and research fields by working as an intervention specialist/mental health paraprofessional (MHPP), autism behavior line therapist, program assistant, and research assistant.

When she is not working full-time as an IT business analyst and adjunct professor, she is working with clients through her public health consulting firm, TF Solutions Center, LLC. She strives to provide quality work and content to each client; through researching, staying current with health information technology and policy changes, attending training/conferences, and participating in webinars to enhance her skills.

During her free time, she enjoys reading and spending quality time with her son and family. She strives each day to show her son that all things are possible through hard work and determination.

Thoughts on advancing in academia from Ms. Ford: I have always been interested in academia. The true motivation was to show and encourage my students that you don't have to go in a straight line for your career. When I was in school, I was not told that you can have an unconventional route and still be successful. My professors and mentors all were only specific to one direction of the field, although I took advantages of internships in various backgrounds, my professors didn't really encourage that.

My path to entering academia started in graduate school as a graduate assistant at the University of Arkansas Little Rock. I've always had a passion for helping others and that position confirmed that I wanted to delve deeper into academia, especially in the areas where the faculty and staff did not look like me (PWI institutions). After that first initial position, I begin asking my mentors and current professors and adjuncts what were the requirements to become an Adjunct professor while I was still in school. My path to entering academia has been fairly easy because every position in academia that I have obtained, I applied and networked.

Choosing the right type of school and its student profile is important in making a good choice for you, as a professor, in your career. You have to make sure you're positioning yourself well where you will have positive mentorships on your academic journey.

Before you apply for any positions in academia, research that university, tour the campus to see for yourself if the vibes match your vibes. Tour the departments/areas that you're interested in working in. Also, do not be afraid to ask questions, interview the staff, students, etc., because you have to make sure this career move is your best move.

The type of school and student profile has to match what you're looking for, you have to make sure that not only you're a good fit, but they're a good fit for you as well.

I wanted to also provide mentorship and encourage my students to think outside of the box, to truly dissect what they're passionate about and where they want to be in their future career. And with that being said, you can find public health in EVERYTHING! Although the position may not directly say public health, indirectly the job duties and responsibilities have relative qualities that you can utilize in that field.

I want to be the gatekeeper for my students/mentees and help them with their blueprint for career success. What inspires me and energizes me as a professor are my students. When I'm able to assist or provide resources to help them in continuing their education, which inspires me that I'm making a real difference. That I am helping lay the foundation for the next up and coming scientists, teachers, professors, researchers, trainers, etc. I've always wanted to help people, growing up my dream was to become a Cardiovascular Surgeon; however those weren't in my cards, but I'm thankful that I have found my purpose.

My purpose was to help educate others in reaching their full potential! I am able to do that by being a college professor, I am able to show other Black women that they can achieve whatever goals they set for themselves. Being the gatekeeper of resources as a professor inspires and energizes me.

I have not encountered any hurdles during my performance evaluations. So far my performance evaluations have been really good! My mentor professor has provided great feedback for me to continue to be successful as an adjunct professor. I also ask a lot of questions to get feedback to show that I am easy to talk to and that I handle constructive criticism well.

Gender has impacted my faculty experience because there are still not as many women—black women especially—that are on the tenure-track. However there are women in leadership roles at my university, so I have not experienced discrimination based on my gender. My race is impacting my faculty experience because I do not have anyone that looks like me—race or gender—that are tenure-track. My mentors at the university I teach at are limited to a specific race. I have Black mentors but they are at other colleges and universities. So if I need to vent or run ideas about my department there is no one that looks like me that could relate to what I'm feeling. I have not experienced discrimination, but at times I still feel limited to share or express my views because I don't have anyone that looks like me in the leadership positions.

Continue to work hard, take advantage of free courses offered to enhance your skills, and know your worth. Do not be afraid to speak up, if they are not listening to you; take your skills and talents, elsewhere. Remember you must advocate for yourself.

As far as balancing all of these professional considerations with other aspects of my life, I'm a single parent so I have to make sure that I'm spending time with my toddler while I am home so I won't do any research, school work such as grading or replying to emails until he is asleep, if I'm not too tired myself.

While I'm working at my full-time job on my breaks, I will work on my research, or leave my desk to make phone calls and reply to emails from my phone in the car.

If I have had a busy week, my weekends, for the most part, are my relaxing days. I clean my home thoroughly, do my grocery shopping, spend time with family, go to church, etc. Meet with friends when I can. However, I've learned that it is acceptable to say "no" and not feel guilty.

I balance being productive but also not neglecting myself or my son/family. Having balance is very important. My beliefs are that you cannot be so engulfed in work that you miss out on enjoying life. Yes, I have to provide for my son and I, but I still want to be able to look back and enjoy seeing him grow up and cherishing moments with my family.

The biggest challenge so far is me not being able to go back to school to pursue my doctorate degree. I know that the only way I can move into a tenured faculty tracked position is I would need to have my Ph.D. so that I could be in the running for a tenure-tracked position. Currently, I cannot afford to go back to school and quit my full-time job to focus on my studies. However, I am considering the option of going to school part-time for my doctorate, I am just researching ways that I can go back to school without paying for it. However, my biggest success so far is me being a mom, a business owner, and an adjunct professor.

I define success by having an opportunity to wake up each morning, with a sound mind and able body. Success to me is it taking one day at a time; I'm not where I was yesterday, so therefore I am successful. My success isn't focused on materialistic things, don't get me wrong having nice things is great, however, I measure my success on the improvement of myself and how I have made a positive impact on someone else. The only thing I would have done differently in my career thus far is have networked more and ask more questions in the beginning.

I don't believe in comparing my success with someone else's success. Because we all are unique, your way of success may not work for me and the same for you in return. The only person I am in competition with is me; I know how to push myself! I love seeing other's success as motivation to keep pushing, but I don't compare.

I define success as small tokens each day that builds into a big success story. Each day that you're alive and well is a success because you have another opportunity to be great in whatever you set your mind to do.

Do not be afraid to step outside of the box, continue to challenge yourself, to learn more, and obtain hands-on opportunities. Do not be afraid to sell yourself, have confidence. No one will believe you're capable of more unless you believe it yourself. Become a subject matter expert in your area of expertise. You are the resource. Continue to network, build your career portfolio, and seek mentors that are at the career level you're trying to obtain. Do not be afraid to ask questions.

Career Shift into Academia

Dr. Tiffany L. Brown is an African-American woman from the Bronx, New York who holds a Ph.D. in child and family studies from Syracuse University, an MA in social sciences and a BS in Psychobiology from Binghamton University. Currently, she teaches in the Family and Consumer Sciences Department at California State University, Long Beach. Her research interests include contextual influences on developmental outcomes for ethnic minority adolescents as well as parenting and socialization practices in African American families. Dr. Brown has been a member of The National Council on Family Relations (NCFR) for fifteen years and has served as former secretary/treasurer for their Ethnic Minority Section and as is currently serving as a member of their Inclusion Diversity Committee.

Thoughts on advancing in academia from Dr. Brown: While I was doing my master's degree, I had three faculty members tell me that they thought I should continue for my Ph.D. One professor sat me down and said that being an academic provided her with a nice life and a great deal of flexibility. I had a very supportive and encouraging group of mentors in this master's program and they gave me a great deal of confidence to continue with my graduate studies. Also during this time, I began meeting with the vice provost on Friday afternoons. He was an African American man, who encouraged students of color to go to graduate school. He helped me to research Ph.D. programs and explained that there were a lot of benefits to being in academia. Again, echoing the sentiments of the other faculty from the department I was in at the time.

Success to me is living life with integrity and balance. I do not think it is about having the most of anything (money, status, power, etc.). It is more about having a balance of things that challenge you, at the same time as having things that come naturally for you. It is having intense moments in your day that are mellowed out by enough peace in the day. I think we have become way too consumed by getting more and I see a lot of people lacking balance. They become sick and unhappy. I see this in academia often. It is a profession that can breed a sense of not being good enough. These ideas get planted in your doctoral program and are continuously nurtured throughout the tenure and promotion process. The academy has done a great job of getting a workforce of very bright people at a low cost to do more than what they should be doing. The expectations are always ambiguous enough that you are constantly questioning where you stand. If this were a romantic relationship, it would be put in the category of dysfunctional.

I do struggle with getting my research out because I teach a lot, often taking adjunct positions on the side to supplement my income. I am single and do not have any support so I have to hustle. I feel like if I didn't have to work year-round, I could publish more and be more marketable. Publishing is key. So, I've gotten dinged in the review process because of my publication record.

Beyond academia, I have given several talks within the community to groups of young people on self-care, career pathways, and developing positive healthy relationships. I was also the vice president of the board of directors for a center serving homeless pregnant women and am currently serving on an advisory board to an organization that provides nutritional, employment, and educational services to women and children. Lastly, I volunteer with a community-based organization in Long Beach, CA that provides gardening and STEM experiences for urban youth. At the national level, I've served on several committees for the national council on family relations and have been an active member of their ethnic minority constituency.

During undergrad, I was pre-med and had hopes of becoming a psychiatrist or a neurologist. By my senior year, I was pretty beat up by my science courses and worried if I could hack med school, so I decided not to take the MCAT and not pursue medicine—I regret that choice. After I graduated with a BS in Organismic Psychobiology, I had zero job prospects in that field and wasn't qualified to do much of anything. However, because I had some psychology and child development training from my major, I was able to land a job as a case manager working with children and families in the foster care and adoption system. I worked in this position for a year and then decided to go back to my undergrad institution for a master's degree. I wanted to do social work but they did not have that option at the time so I decided to get a degree in social sciences and human development. It was a great program with a supportive faculty, but it wasn't the most strategic degree. After I completed my masters, I went back to the foster care and adoption agency I had previously been employed by and became a supervisor of caseworkers. I worked in that position for a year and a half and then decided to do my Ph.D. Which led to my first job as an adjunct faculty (2 years) and then my first full-time tenure track position in 2003. Now that I'm here, I'm most inspired by the fact that students who want to learn. The curiosity of students to learn more about themselves and others.

Gender and race have influenced my career. I was always told that you shouldn't start a family until you have tenure. I put a lot of emphasis on my career early and never had children. If I had to do it again I would have been more open to having children despite my stage in the tenure process. I wish I would have focused more on my relationships and built that part of my life rather than worrying so much about tenure.

As a faculty of color, you tend to do more service than your colleagues who are not of color. You are usually one of the few people on campus that serve as a mentor to students of color and you get asked to be the "person of color" on every committee. Also for many people of color, collectivism is central to our value system, so service is natural for us, but this is not always valued in academia. There is a great deal of competition so it can also feel like you are not energetically in-tune with the culture of academia as it differs so much from one's home culture.

Work-life integration can be a challenge. You always feel like you could be doing work. But you have to create boundaries so that you can take care of yourself. It is easy to get sucked into the academic mind-frame that starts in grad school of "always working." I took my work email off of my personal cell phone and I tell students that I do not answer emails in the evenings or on weekends. I make sure to get to the gym or yoga 5 times a week and I usually do not compromise that. I also strive to get at least 7 hours of sleep each night. For teaching, I have converted some of my courses to online or hybrid as it frees me up a little more so that I can get chunks of time in for writing.

To get practical about pursuing a career in academia, it is important to remember that even if a school is a "teaching institution" you will need to have an active program of research. So, make sure you stay on top of that. Don't think that choosing a teaching institution will mean you aren't expected to publish. In my experience, the teaching institutions that I've worked for have slowly moved towards research-intensive because that brings in the money. At a public institution, there are constant budget cuts that influence the level of support that is available and your salary. I was at a public institution and got furloughed because they had state budget issues. The budget can also impact the number of people that receive promotion in a given year and new faculty hires. Not having faculty hires when they are needed puts more work on the current faculty. Especially in small departments, you can wind up having to serve on every committee because there just aren't enough hands on deck. I also believe I should have done a postdoc. I was so tired of being broke and living like a college student at the age of thirty that I took an academic job right out of my doctoral program. I needed to expand my network and also to cultivate my research skills in a postdoctoral fellowship and I regret not doing one.

Once in the classroom, I recommend making the material relatable to the personal lives of students. I also share a lot about my personal life as examples of course content. Additionally, I invite my students to volunteer with me in the community.

For better chances for success on this journey, get strong mentors and write collaboratively with others who are also seeking tenure and promotion as they have the same level of motivation to get stuff out. Sometimes it's good to work with folks who are already full professor because they have experience and connections, but remember they are not really motivated to get stuff out, so projects can sit for long periods with them. Also, choose your service wisely. Do something at the department level, college level, and university level that will not drain you. Ask more seasoned faculty for suggestions on which committees to serve on. Do not feel like you need to be on everything. Service does not get you tenure or promotion.

Though my larger challenges are getting federal grants and publishing, my largest success is my reputation as a teacher. Students have always been vocal about how I have made a difference in their lives. I strive to give them the support and guidance that I needed at their stage.

Do quality work that can make a difference in the real world. I think community involvement goes a long way. Also, if you find an issue that your campus community is dealing with and develop research and programming around that issue while involving students, that is a huge win! I know one faculty member who decided to tackle student homelessness and food insecurity and this has made her very visible on campus. Meanwhile, she is doing a great deal of good for our students.

Get educated at an institution that can broaden your network and support your growth. Choose your degree carefully, be strategic about it. It is important to like the area that you choose but also to ensure that you are not limited to too narrow of scope and that you remain marketable.

Tenured and Tenacious

Ndidiamaka N. Amutah-Onukagha received her Ph.D. in public

health with a focus on maternal and child health from the University of Maryland, College Park School of Public Health in 2010. She received her Master's in Public Health from The George Washington University School of Public Health and Health Services in Maternal and Child Health in 2005. Dr. Amutah-Onukagha also received a BS in Public Health and a BA in Africana Studies from Rutgers, The State University of NJ. Ndidiamaka has a longstanding commitment to public health that spans over fifteen years of experience. Her current research interests include health disparities, reproductive health, infant mortality, and HIV/AIDS in ethnic minority populations. Ndidiamaka is a member of the American Public Health Association and is currently the co-chair of the Perinatal and Women's Health committee in the Maternal and Child Health section.

Dr. Amutah-Onukagha is a former president of The Society of African American Public Health Issues (SAAPHI) and currently serves on the board of directors for the National Women's Health Network. Additionally, Dr. Amutah-Onukagha is an associate professor at the Department of Public Health and Community Medicine at Tufts University School of Medicine. In this capacity, her research focuses on HIV/AIDS and women of color in an urban context, adverse birth outcomes for women of color, and community-based participatory research.

Thoughts on advancing in academia from Dr. Amutah-Onukagha: I have always been curious about differences in health outcomes as experienced by different groups of people and the ability to train future generations of students is very meaningful to me. The ability to shape and train young minds that are destined for greatness is very inspirational for me. I always remember looking back over my academic career and wishing that I had a Black female mentor/faculty member that I could relate to. Now that I am in a position to be a resource for other students, I am energized by this. Further, I define success by meeting my self-defined goals as it relates to my career, family, and life. The beauty of living by my own rules and expectations is that it frees me to move at my own pace without the restrictions of comparison. In my career, I set goals for myself that are time-bound and I work backward from there.

My institution is a good choice for me as a professor for many reasons. It is a private university which provides access to many resources and opportunities for internal funding. Additionally, the salary and overall package offering was very competitive during the recruitment process. Finally, as it is a graduate-level school, all of my research assistants are excited and motivated to participate in research and they are great support for the current studies I am managing. The best advice I can give about connecting with students is to be yourself! Students are like sponges, very excited and eager to learn from you, so your authenticity will be what is most attractive to them. In addition to them being excited about learning from you, they will appreciate you holding them accountable while helping to develop their leadership skills.

While my biggest challenges have been changing the type of institution that I have taught at to grow my career, and moving my family along with me in the process, I have not encountered many hurdles during the performance evaluation and promotion period. I think that a large part of that is due to starting my career at a university that had very clear requirements and expectations for the tenure and promotion process. Overall, most of the academic challenges that occur can be overcome with a good mentoring team, a supportive chair, and some good girlfriends that understand what you are going through.

My race has definitely impacted my faculty experience, in both my assistant and associate professor positions I have been one of the very few faculty members of color in the department and institution. The impact of this has been that I am keenly aware of my race and positioning when taking on leadership positions within the university and department to ensure that each role is balanced and serves as an asset to my overall career trajectory.

Balancing teaching, research, and family commitments require being very organized. I have my dedicated days that I go to campus, meet with students, and write. I am very diligent about protecting those days and times, and people on my research team as well as my colleagues have gotten the memo about my schedule.

My biggest success has been going through the tenure and promotion process at two different universities. The beauty of having a career is that you can always reinvent yourself and do something else. The freedom of that thought gives me much peace. Do good work, be kind, and don't step on the toes of people you collaborate with. Stay true to yourself, trust your gut, and cultivate an amazing team of mentors that will guide you throughout your career.

Intrinsically Inspired

Dr. Maranda Griffin is the director of clinical skills training of Walden University's School of Counseling. She has been highly engaged in the field of behavioral health for the past nineteen years as a state department of mental health director, program director, and practitioner. She couples her state and community expertise with over twenty years of service to our country as a retired equal opportunity director and officer in the Air National Guard. She earned her Ph.D. in Counselor Education from Auburn University, her MA in Counseling and Psychology from Troy University, and her Bachelors in Elementary Education from Troy University.

Thoughts on advancing in academia from Dr. Griffin: I have a Bachelor's degree in Education and as I continued with my educational advancement, academia was among the career options available to me. For me, academia was a natural fit for my preferences and areas in which I thrive. Apart of my personal, teaching, and people philosophy involves a belief that we have untapped potential within us that lies dormant until activated. I believe in academia, I have the capacity to help students activate their maximum potential.

I am intrinsically motivated; so my inspiration comes from within. I am intentional about my personal goals and that energizes me to continue to strive for excellence and to do my best. I consciously recognize that I am among a small minority based on my gender, race, and ethnicity in academia and this awareness contributes to my inspiration to ensure that faculty represent the students they teach.

I define success by ensuring that I live out the purpose for which I was created and that each day I strive towards that purpose not leaving anything on the table that was within my reach to acquire or obtain. I secured my first job in academia as an adjunct professor at the university I was completing doctoral teaching internship hours at. After a semester of internship, the internship converted to a paid internship as an adjunct professor. This job was within the university system of my alma mater. I continued to hold this position for three years until a full-time teaching position restricted me from teaching for another university.

The school I am at currently is a good choice for me as I desire to work from home so that I may also commit my time to parent an eighteen-month-old. If I were working in a traditional setting I would not have the amount of time that I currently have at home to devote myself to parenting.

The best advice I have to connect with students as a faculty member is to be yourself and to fully stand in who you are as yourself. Students will readily identify your values and who you are as a person from the example that you live before them. During my doctoral studies, a faculty member of the majority gender and race encouraged me to do this and at first, I did not recognize why he was doing this. Later, I understood that it was not necessary for me to assimilate into the persona of what I thought the majority would accept but to recognize that there was a place for me at the table.

The only hurdles I have encountered with performance evaluation are limited to salary increase restrictions imposed by the university. In the point-based evaluation system, there is a threshold associated with the salary increase and the university seems to try to keep faculty under that threshold as a justification to keep raises capped. In promotion consideration, I compete when opportunities arise that seem to be a good fit for me. Hurdles that exist with these opportunities are having specific individuals in mind for the position that could discourage application. There will always be the potential for external hurdles but never allow those hurdles to distort your internal drive. Hurdles are meant to be ascended, so jump.

Concerning gender and race, I am not cognizant of how gender has impacted my faculty experience as the majority of those I work with are the same gender as I am. Systemic racism is prevalent in our country and this racism often appears covertly in the workplace. While I do not have explicit examples, as a woman of color, there is always a type of questioning that occurs based on my worldview within the academic setting. I can easily look at the demographic factors of the student body and not see those demographic factors equally represented in faculty and most certainly not in equivocal leadership roles.

My biggest challenges so far have been securing an online faculty position. It seemed to take some time to secure an online faculty position because of the high interest in these positions.

How do I get things done? I utilize a planner, tasks lists, and a set work schedule to assist with balance. I identify research goals for the year and I do not overtask or deviate from that goal for the year. It is easy to get pulled into additional research that is outside of your own targets. I go back to my own goals for myself to aid me in when to say yes and when to say no. I adhere to a traditional work schedule and outside of that schedule, I do not work. I also block time on my work calendar to exhale, take a break, and to stretch.

There are enough antagonists out there, don't be your own antagonist. If you have a goal to advance in academia, articulate that goal, set strategies to support reaching that goal, and pursue that goal!

Just Do It

Think carefully about the rank to which you initially apply. Once you are hired at this rank, there is no turning back. All promotion and advancement will be based on the chosen rank. If you are applying to a school that offers both lecturer and professor positions, understand the credentials of faculty who have been hired for each to assure fair pay and placement. Believe in yourself and your capabilities. Understand competitive pay for the position to which you have applied. Always negotiate your salary when possible, though there may be constraints in the public university pay structure.

Universities often hire a full school year in advance, such that the hiring committee can receive applications during the Fall semester, interview during the Spring semester, and hire for the following Fall semester. In some cases, the full application and hiring process can take place in the Spring or Summer before. Prepare your materials during the Summer in time for Fall job postings.

For universities and organizations seeking to hire a diverse workforce, remember that women of color are not a monolith. As illustrated by the stories herein, Black women are not a monolith and some believe race and gender influenced their career trajectory and others did not believe so. African-American women and African women in America may indeed relate to academia quite differently. Race is a social construct and is not interchangeable with ethnicity. Different cultures have a difference in collective histories that shape their experiences in the workplace. Levels of acculturation and assimilation directly influence experiences of marginalization in the workplace. Location of the school geographically and the orientation of the school politically also influence cultural acceptance.

All women should be respected for their character and knowledge, regardless of, and in honor of, our differences that shape our rich stories. We share this American perspective in hopes of strengthening diversity and inclusion domestically and inspiring global conversations regarding the American academic experience abroad.

Your career longevity in academia depends on your patience, perseverance, and dedication to higher education in an ivory tower climate that struggles with diversity and inclusion in many cases. Advancing and succeeding in academia is as much about your credentials as it is your character. Build a brand through conferences, consulting, articles, and teaching that reflects you; and illustrate that you are a resource to audiences and communities globally. Implementing the strategies from this book will allow you to gain successful entry and advancement. Get started.

The beauty of the academy is what you are able to bring to the table and how you are able to benefit from what is already on the table for you. Cultivate a network of other Black women that you can confide in, collaborate with, and celebrate mutual achievements both within and outside of the academy together. *The Black Women Faculty Connection*, our online community, is a great start to engage with like-minded women on the journey. Consistency, confidence, and character are the keys to success and are essential to making the most out of the path that you have chosen.

CPSIA information can be obtained
at www.ICGtesting.com
Printed in the USA
BVHW071054191119
564177BV00019B/1745/P